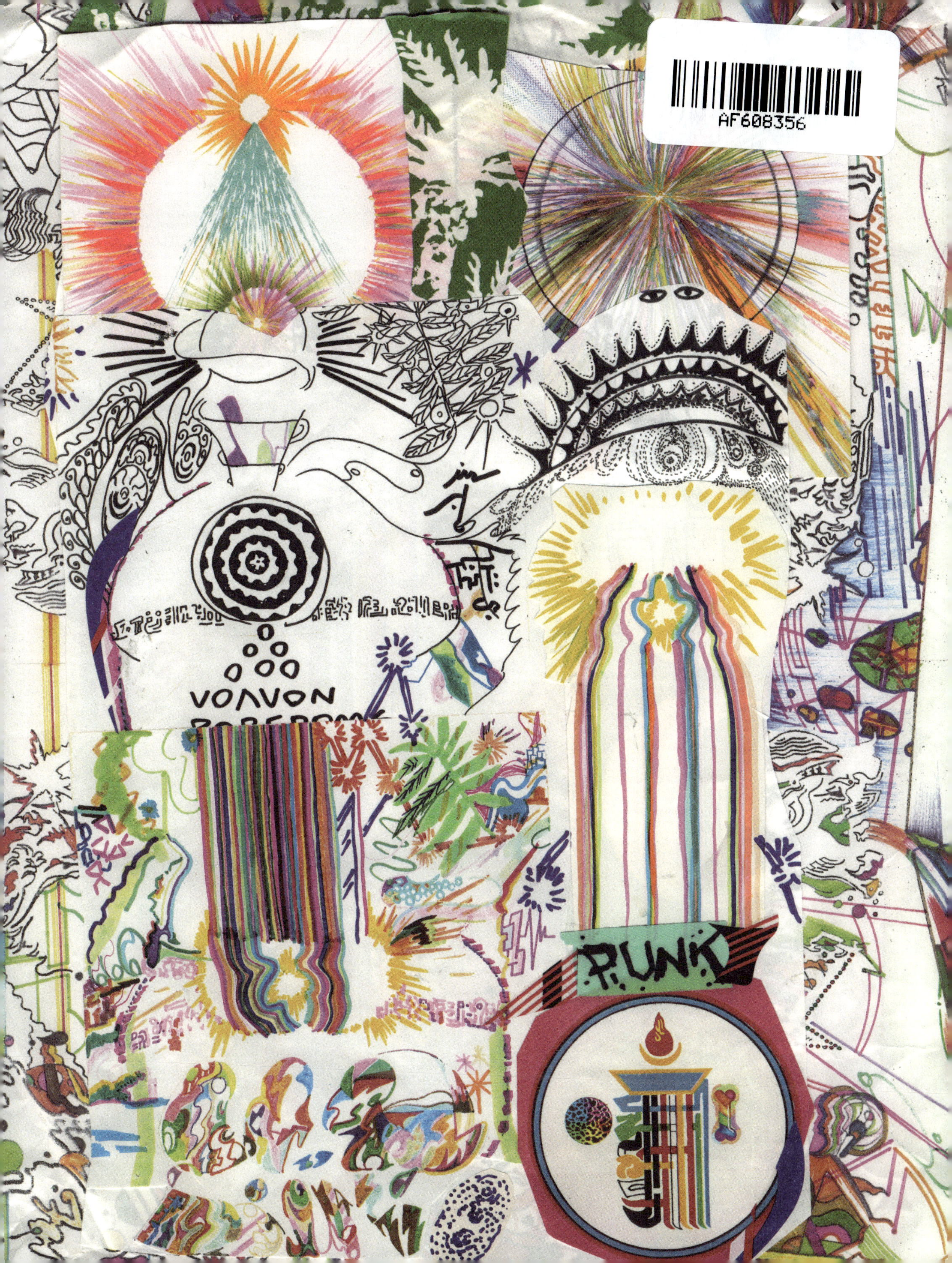
AF608356
VONVON
PUNK

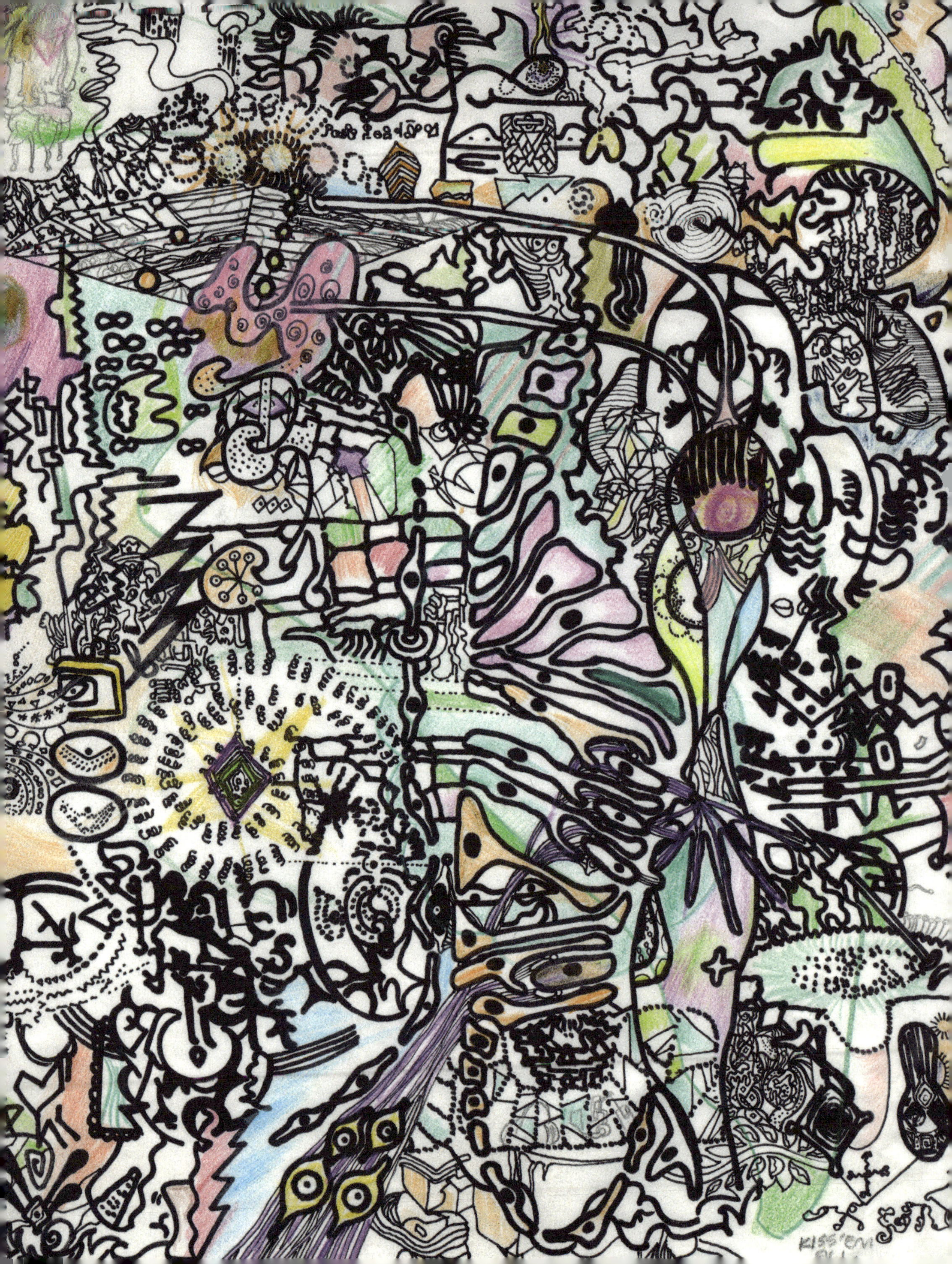
KISS'EM

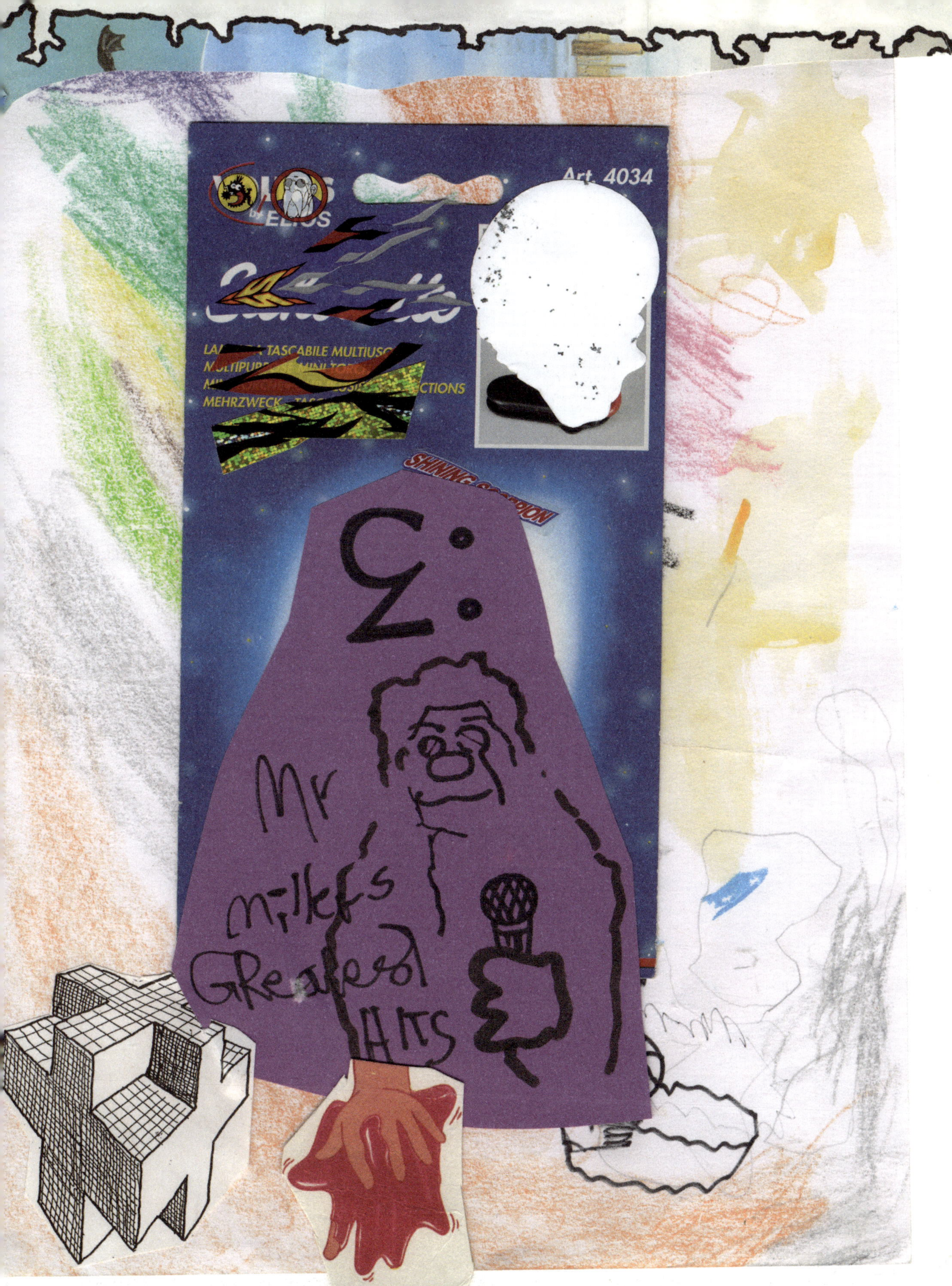
Art. 4034
ELIOS
TASCABILE MULTIUSO
MEHRZWECK
Mr Miller's Greatest Hits

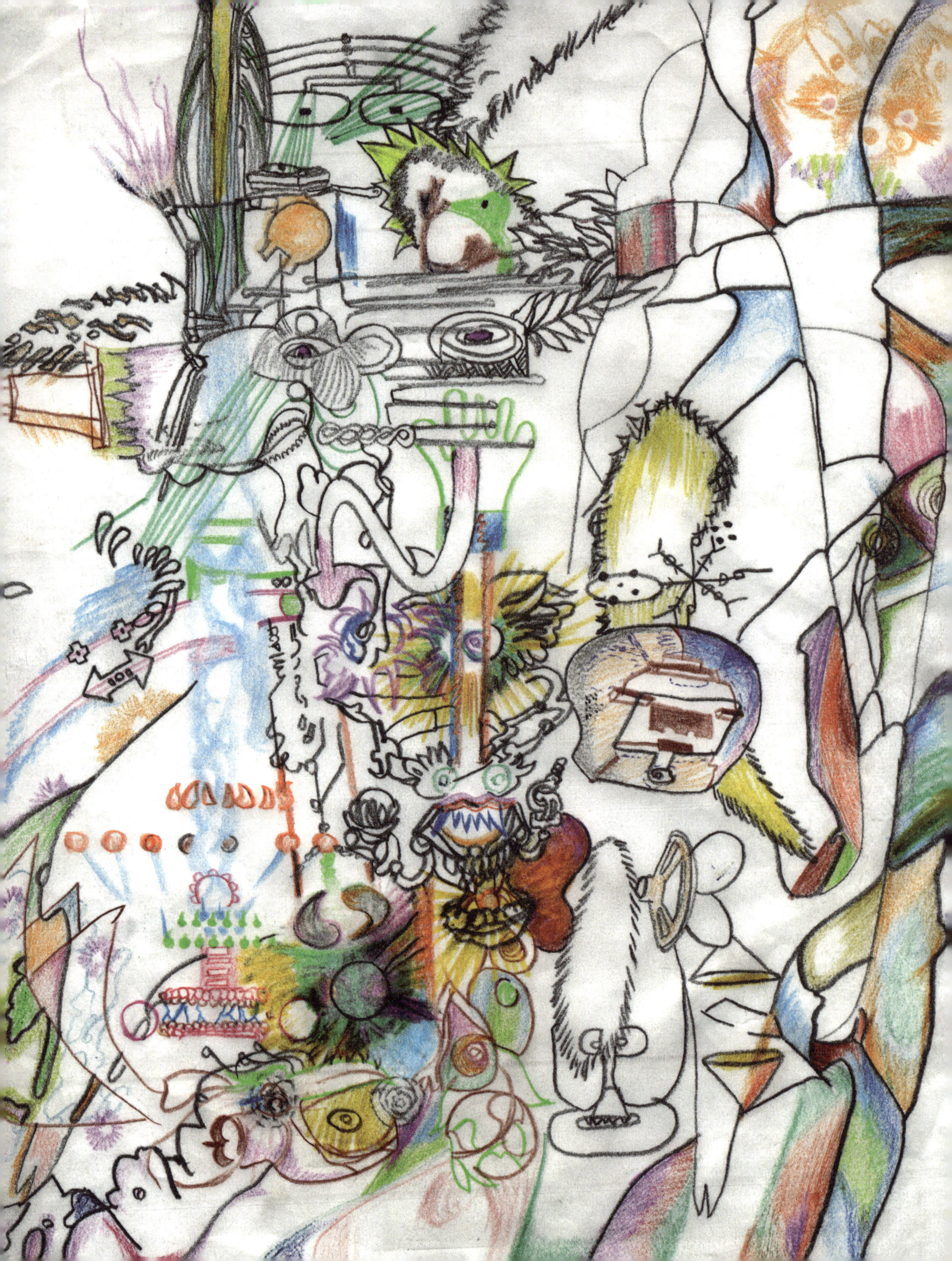

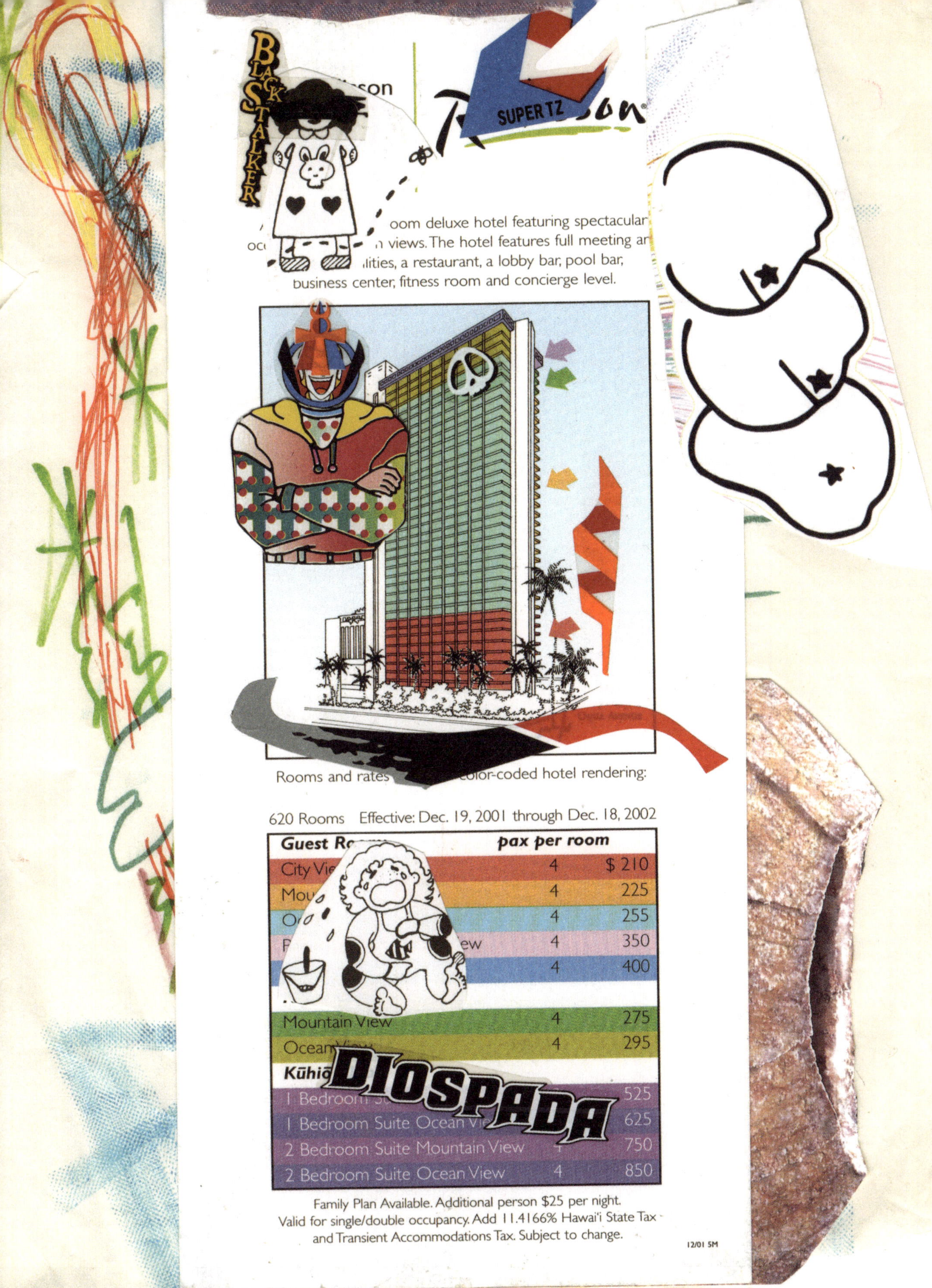
BLACK STALKER
SUPER TZ
oom deluxe hotel featuring spectacular
n views. The hotel features full meeting an
ilities, a restaurant, a lobby bar, pool bar,
business center, fitness room and concierge level.
Rooms and rates
color-coded hotel rendering:
620 Rooms Effective: Dec. 19, 2001 through Dec. 18, 2002
pax per room
City Vie 4 $ 210
4 225
4 255
ew 4 350
4 400
Mountain View 4 275
Ocean View 4 295
DIOSPADA
525
1 Bedroom Suite Ocean Vi 625
2 Bedroom Suite Mountain View 4 750
2 Bedroom Suite Ocean View 4 850
Family Plan Available. Additional person $25 per night.
Valid for single/double occupancy. Add 11.4166% Hawai'i State Tax
and Transient Accommodations Tax. Subject to change.
12/01 5M

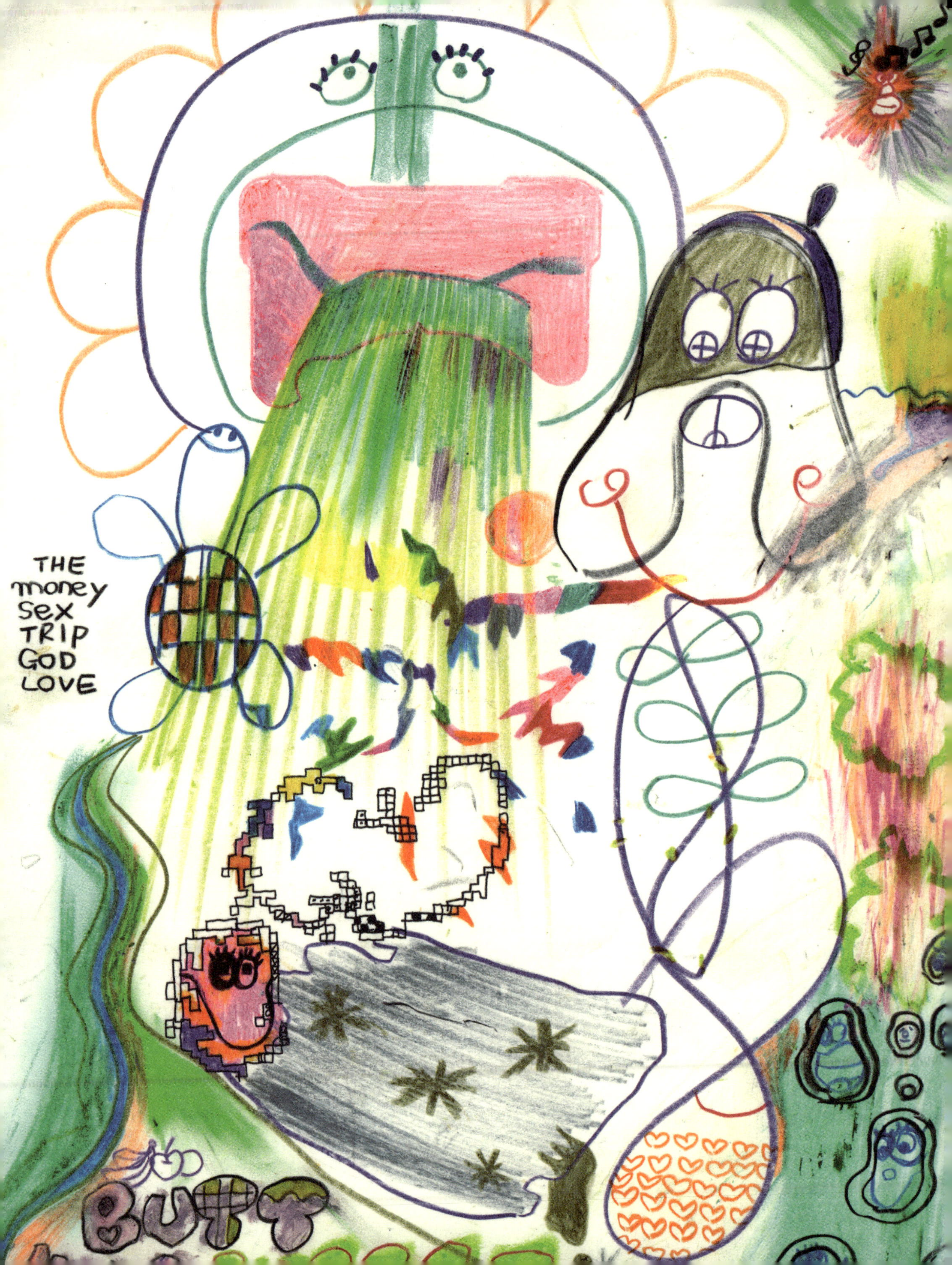
THE
money
sex
TRIP
GOD
LOVE
BUTT

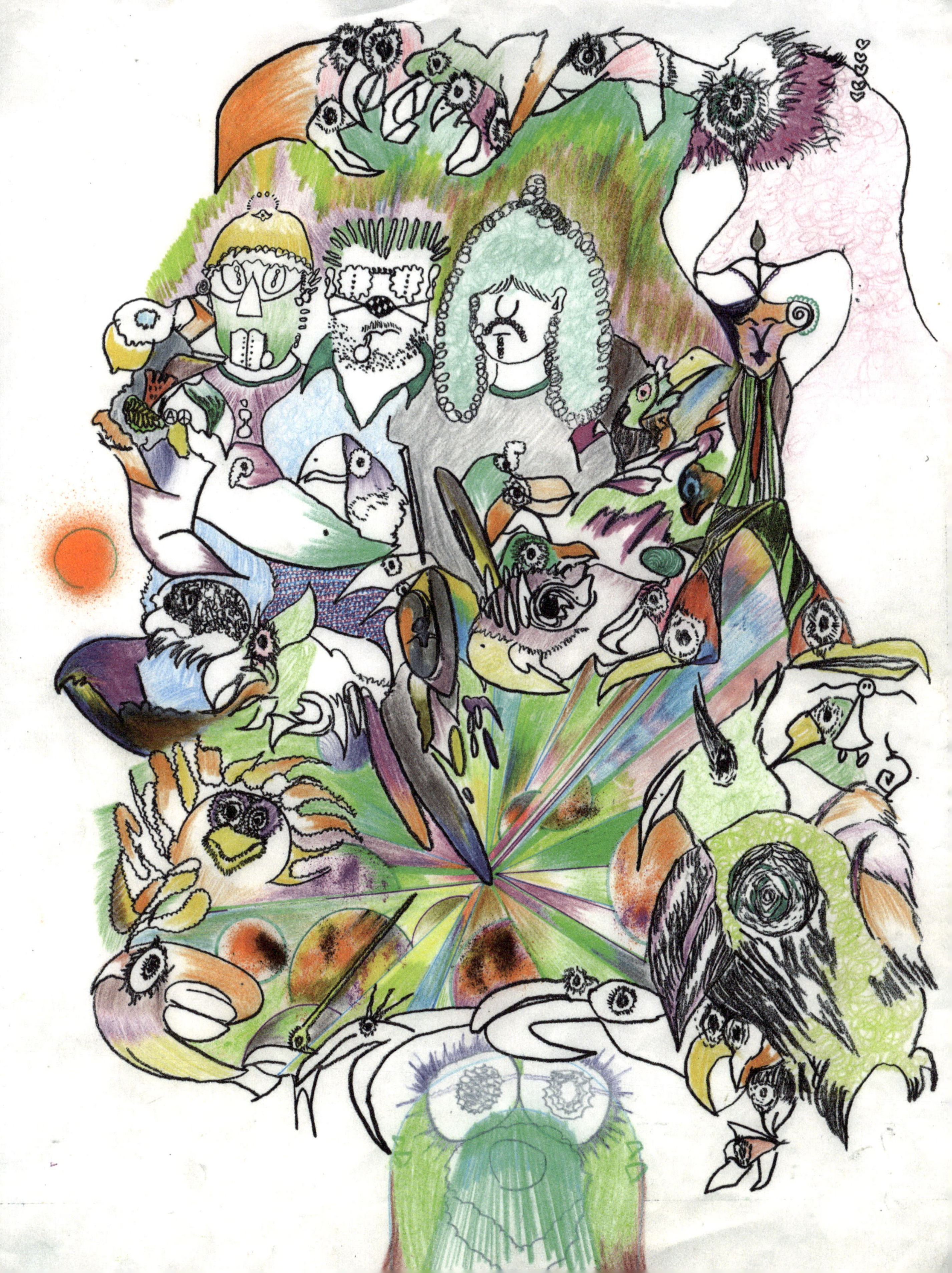

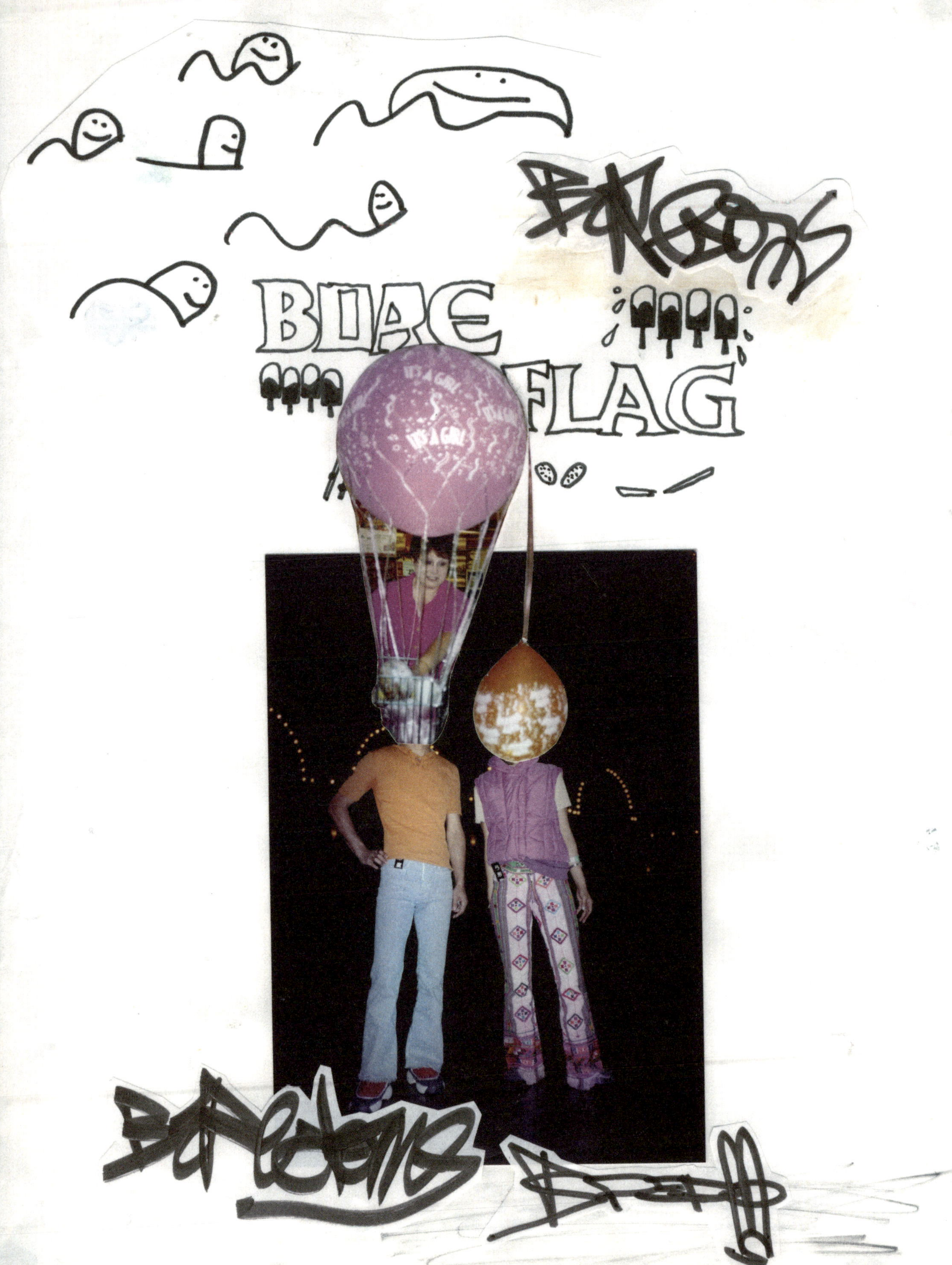
BLAC
FLAG
IT'S A GIRL!

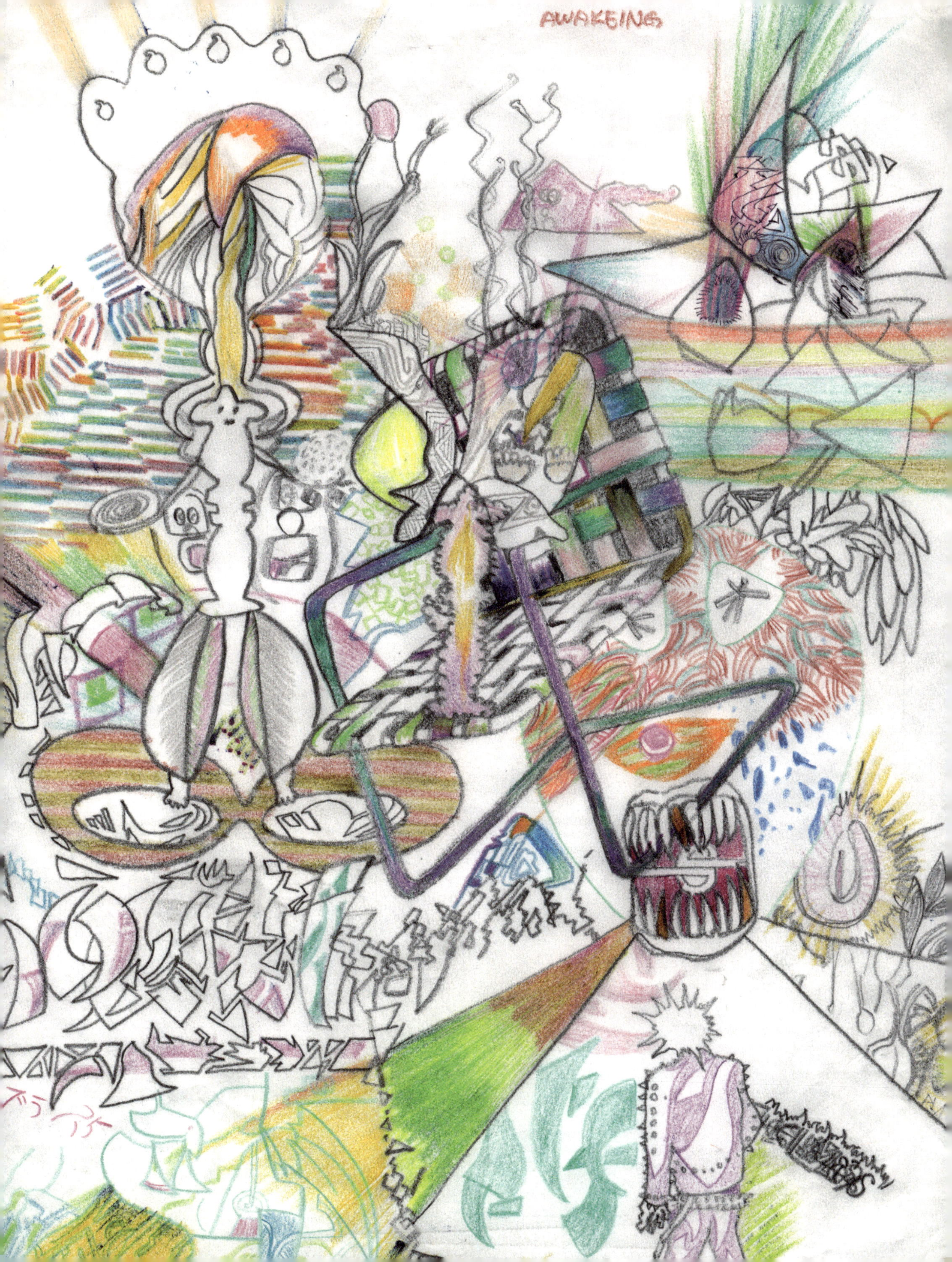
AWAKEING

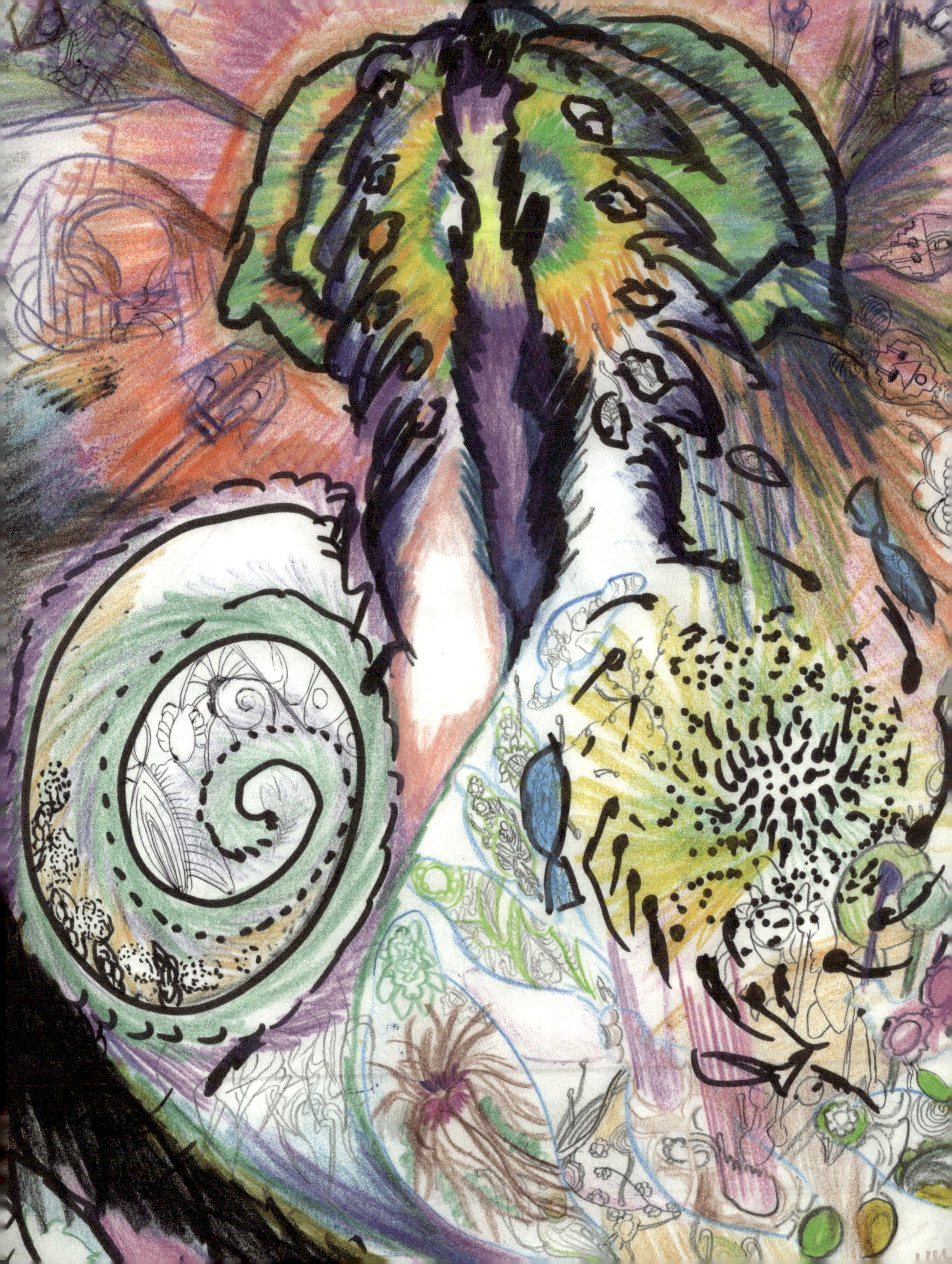

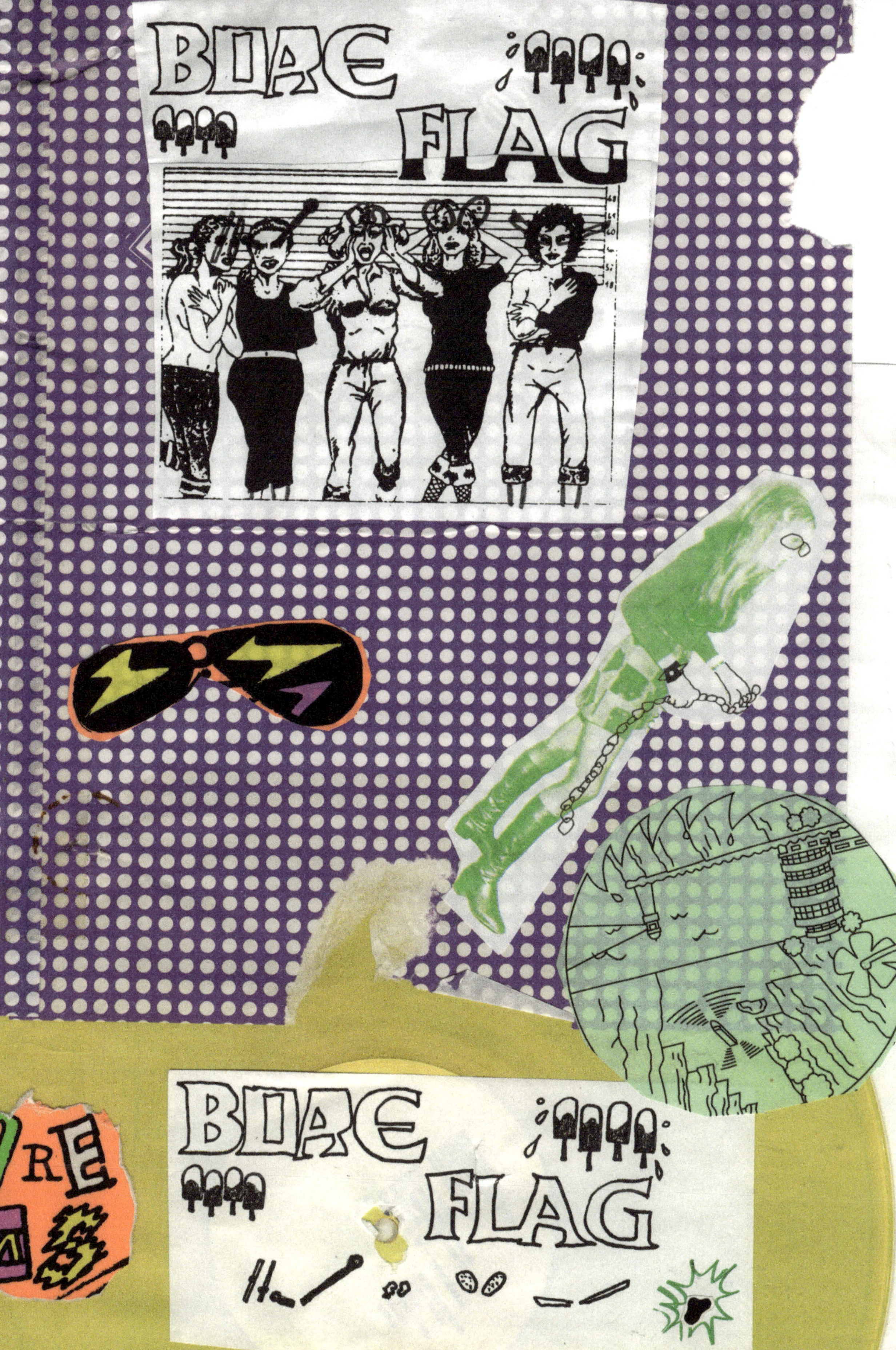
BORE FLAG
BORE FLAG
BORE doms

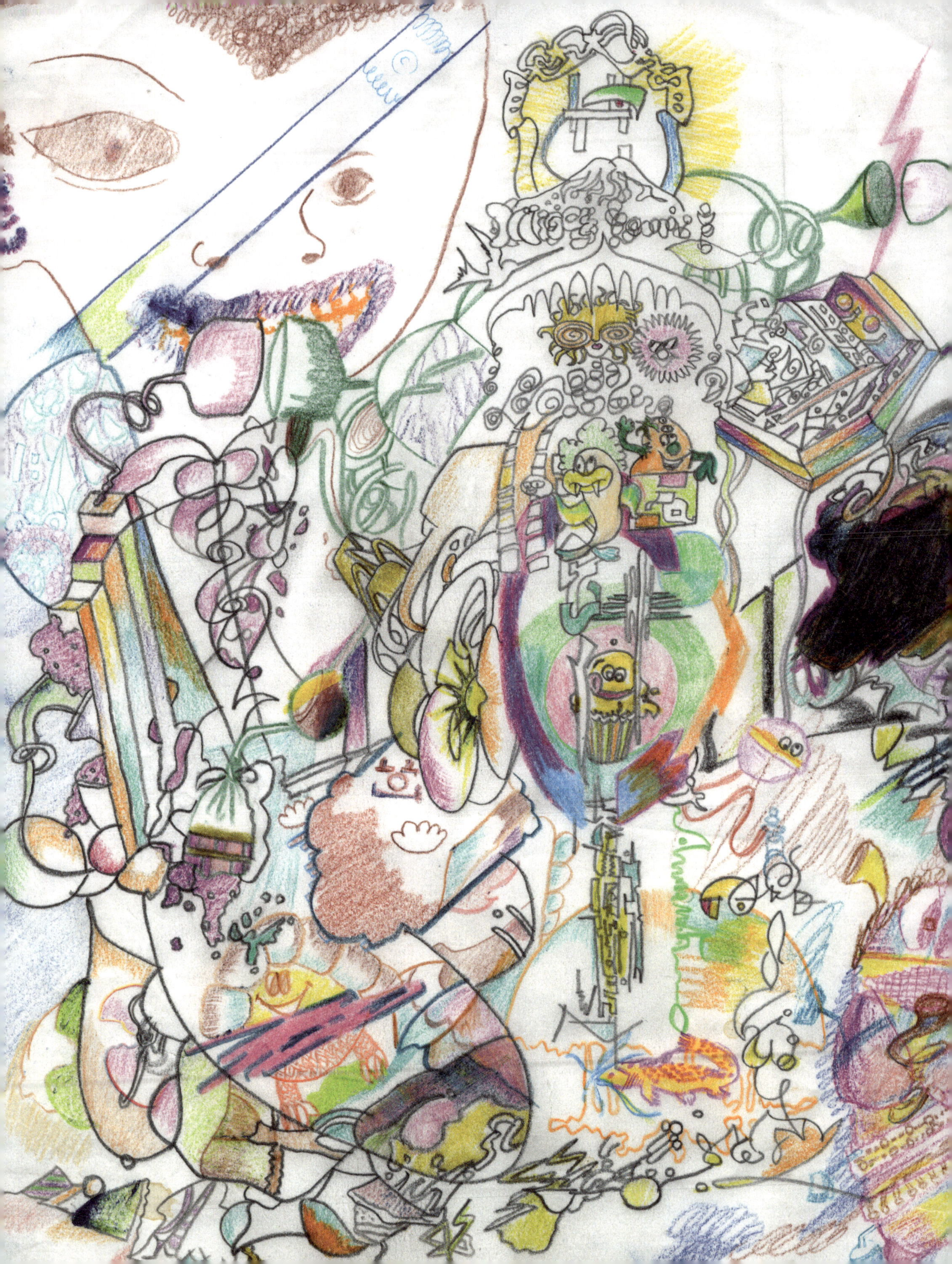